IMPERIAL
1964 THROUGH 1968
PHOTO ARCHIVE

IMPERIAL
1964 THROUGH 1968
PHOTO ARCHIVE

Photographs from the
Iconografix Collection of Automotive Images and
Chrysler Historical Foundation

Edited with introduction by
P. A. Letourneau

Iconografix
Photo Archive Series

Iconografix
P.O. Box 18433
Minneapolis, Minnesota 55418 USA

Library of Congress Card Number 94-78695

ISBN 1-882256-23-9

94 95 96 97 98 99 00 5 4 3 2 1

Cover and book design by Lou Gordon, Osceola, Wisconsin

Printed in the United States of America

Book trade distribution by Voyageur Press, Inc. (800) 888-9653

PREFACE

The histories of machines and mechanical gadgets are contained in the books, journals, correspondence and personal papers stored in libraries and archives throughout the world. Written in tens of languages, covering thousands of subjects, the stories are recorded in millions of words.

Words are powerful. Yet, the impact of a single image, a photograph or an illustration, often relates more than dozens of pages of text. Fortunately, many of the libraries and archives that house the words also preserve the images.

In the *Photo Archive Series*, Iconografix reproduces photographs and illustrations selected from public and private collections. The images are chosen to tell a story—to capture the character of their subject. Reproduced as found, they are accompanied by the captions made available by the archive.

The Iconografix *Photo Archive Series* is dedicated to young and old alike, the enthusiast, the collector and anyone who, like us, is fascinated by "things" mechanical.

Rendering of a 1966 Imperial Crown Two Door Hardtop.

6

INTRODUCTION

Tail fins, expansive front grilles, and an abundance of chrome trim were pronounced elements of Imperial's styling from 1957 through 1963, just as they were characteristic of nearly every American automobile design of the period. While we now look back at such excess with fondness, by the early 1960s American tastes were changing. Leading the luxury car market into the new decade was the 1961 Lincoln Continental. Continental offered an understated elegance that appealed to luxury car buyers in record numbers. Its slab-sided design, with squared-off front and rear, and suicide doors was an unqualified success.

Chrysler responded to Continental in what might be best described as a "pragmatic" fashion. It hired its chief designer, Elwood P. Engel, to replace Virgil M. Exner, the man responsible for Imperial's distinctive styling of the late 1950s and early 1960s. The first Engel designed Chryslers appeared for the 1963 model year, yet changes to Imperial were limited. In 1964, however, the Imperial was dramatically restyled. Imperial lost its tail fins and gained a squared-off silhouette that reflected the influence of Continental. Other changes in 1964 included the elimination of the Custom, introduced in 1959, as Imperial's base model.

With the exception of a new four door Crown sedan in 1966 and the introduction of a shorter wheelbase and unit body construction in 1967, Imperial styling was not radically changed in the years 1964 through 1968. The most notable mechanical change of the period was the introduction of the 350 horsepower, 440 cubic inch V8 engine in 1966.

A book about design, rather than a review of mechanics, *Imperial 1964 through 1968 Photo Archive* explores the elegance of Imperial, in contrast to that of Continental, through two series of factory photographs comparing the features of both four door and two door models. To complete the study of the period, additional photographs and illustrations are offered from both the Iconografix Collection of Automotive Images and the Chrysler Historical Collection.

1964

IMPERIAL CROWN AND LeBARON

Left and right side views of the 1964 Imperial Crown Four Door Hardtop.

10

Front and rear views of the 1964 Crown Four Door Hardtop.

12

Interior views of the 1964 Crown Four Door Hardtop.

Engel versus Engel— Imperial versus Lincoln Continental. In the following pages Elwood Engel's two most popular designs are compared and contrasted in a series of Chrysler factory photos.

18

Imperial's more conventional four door configuration as compared to the Continental's trademark suicide doors.

20

Views of the interiors of the 1964 Imperial Crown Four Door Hardtop and the 1964 Lincoln Continental.

Fill-er-up! The 1964 Crown Four Door Hardtop at the pump.

A drive through the suburbs in a 1964 Imperial Crown Four Door Hardtop.

28

1964 Imperial Crown Coupe Two Door Hardtop with vinyl roof, a $91.20 option.

1964 Imperial Crown Convertible. *Chrysler Historical Collection*

1964 Crown Convertible. *Chrysler Historical Collection*

Left and right hand views of the 1964 Imperial LeBaron. *Chrysler Historical Collection*

1965

IMPERIAL CROWN AND LeBARON

A 1965 Imperial Crown Four Door Hardtop.

The 1965 Crown Four Door Hardtop photographed with a 1965 Lincoln Continental, 1965 Chrysler New Yorker, and a 1965 Plymouth Fury.

Comparing the 1965 Crown Four Door Hardtop and the 1965 Lincoln Continental.

Pointing out the glass panel that covered the headlights of the 1965 Imperial.

The 1965 Crown Four Door Hardtop dashboard.

1965 Crown Four Door Hardtop with leather trim interior, a $104.30 option.

On the road with the 1965 Imperial Crown Four Door Hardtop.

48

Envy of the neighborhood! A proud owner shows off his new Imperial.

Left and right hand views of the 1965 Imperial Crown Coupe Two Door Hardtop.

Chrysler Historical Collection

Left and right hand views of the 1965 Crown Coupe Two Door Hardtop with optional padded roof. *Chrysler Historical Collection*

Crown Coupe interior view. *Chrysler Historical Collection*

Crown Coupe with automatic beam changer, a $46 option. *Chrysler Historical Collection*

On the road with a 1965 Imperial Crown Coupe Two Door Hardtop.

The 1965 Imperial Crown Convertible. *Chrysler Historical Collection*

Two views of the 1965 Imperial Crown Convertible. *Chrysler Historical Collection*

Chrysler Historical Collection

The 1965 Imperial LeBaron photographed at the Chicago Auto Show. *Chrysler Historical Collection*

1966
IMPERIAL CROWN AND LeBARON

Rendering of a 1966 Imperial Crown Four Door Hardtop.

Right and left hand views of a 1966 Imperial Crown Four Door Hardtop.

Views of the rear and trunk of the 1966 Crown Four Door Hardtop.

The 1966 Imperial featured Chrysler's 440 cubic inch, 350 horsepower V-8 engine, as fitted to the New Yorker.

72

Factory tests of the windshield wiper system.

Crown equipped with three-ring whitewall tires, a $54.05 option.

Salesman and customer discuss the merits of the 1966 Crown Four Door Hardtop.

Interior views of the six-way power front bench seat, a $122.35 option on the 1966 Crown Four Door Hardtop.

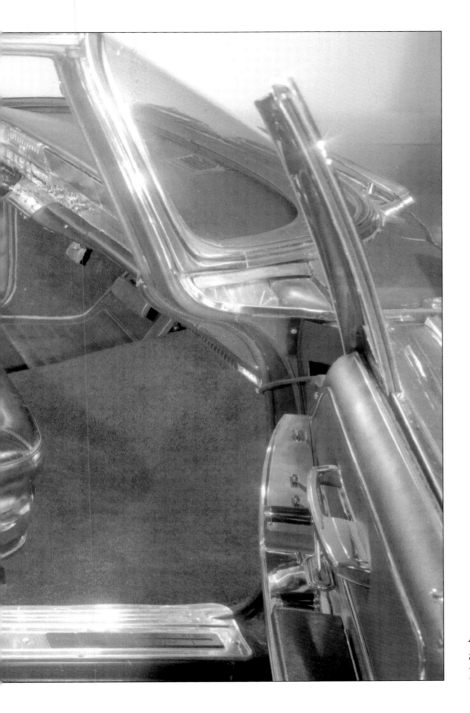

Although production figures dipped in 1966, the luxury of leather and full six-passenger seating made this Imperial Custom Four Door Hardtop a standout.

Two views of the interior of the Custom Four Door Hardtop with optional headrests, split bench seat and leather trim.

While lap seat belts were standard equipment, center passenger and shoulder belts were optional.

Rendering of the Crown Four Door Hardtop with standard cloth interior.

Power brakes were standard equipment on all 1966 Imperials.

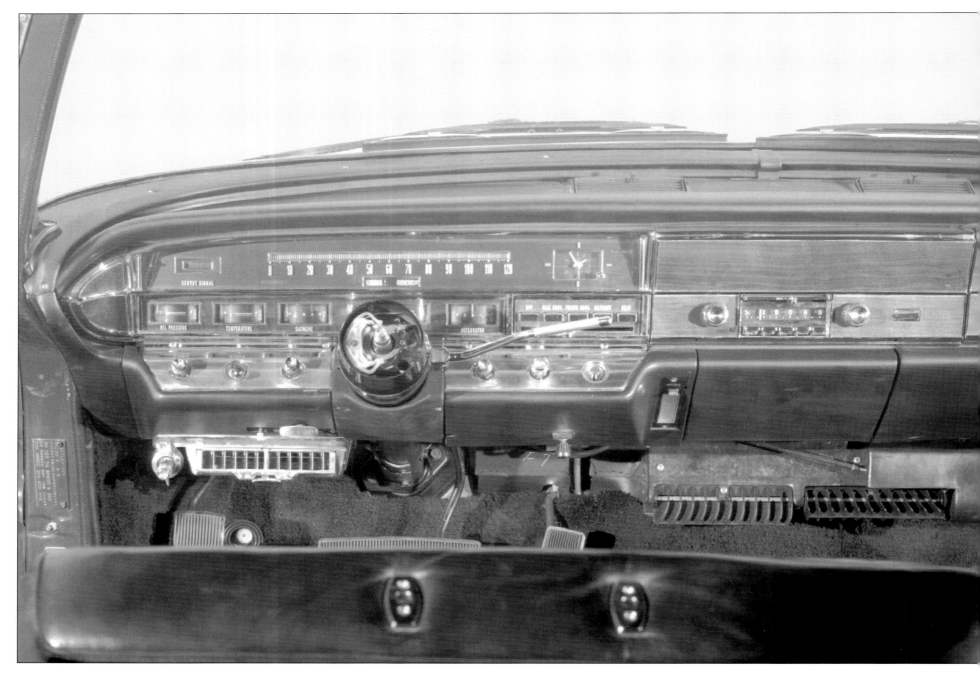

View of the dashboard of the 1966 Crown Four Door Hardtop.

In 1966, the power steering was standard equipment on all Imperials.

90

AM Touch-Tuner radio with rear speaker and power antenna was a $165.45 option.

Air conditioning was a $452.26 option.

Power windows and vent windows were standard equipment on all Imperials in 1966.

94

Six-way power seats were optional on the 1966 Imperial Crown.

Power window and door lock controls on the Crown Four Door Hardtop. Power door locks were a $70.70 option.

The 1966 Imperial Crown Four Door Hardtop and General Motor's top-of-the-line Oldsmobile Ninety-Eight and Buick Electra 225.

The 1966 Crown Four Door Hardtop with optional vinyl roof.

On the road with the 1966 Imperial Crown Four Door Hardtop.

The 1966 Crown Two Door Hardtop.

Side and rear views of the 1966 Crown Two Door Hardtop.

A rematch of Imperial versus Lincoln Continental, this time the 1966 Crown Coupe versus the Continental Coupe.

110

The elegant styling of the 1966 Crown Two Door Hardtop. *Chrysler Historical Collection*

Chrysler Historical Collection

Renderings of the exterior and interior of the 1966 Imperial Crown Convertible.

Chrysler Historical Collection

Rendering of the 1966 Imperial LeBaron Four Door Hardtop.

Front and left side views of the 1966 Imperial LeBaron. *Chrysler Historical Collection*

Chrysler Historical Collection

LeBaron styling was identical to that of the Crown, however, its interior was more plush. *Chrysler Historical Collection*

1967

IMPERIAL CROWN AND LeBARON

Left and right side views of the 1967 Crown Four Door Hardtop. *Chrysler Historical Collection*

In 1967, Imperial employed unit body construction for the first time. *Chrysler Historical Collection*

The 1967 Crown Two Door Hardtop. *Chrysler Historical Collection*

130

Crown Two Door Hardtop with Mobile Director package, a $597.40 option. *Chrysler Historical Collection*

Right and left side views of the 1967 Imperial Convertible. *Chrysler Historical Collection*

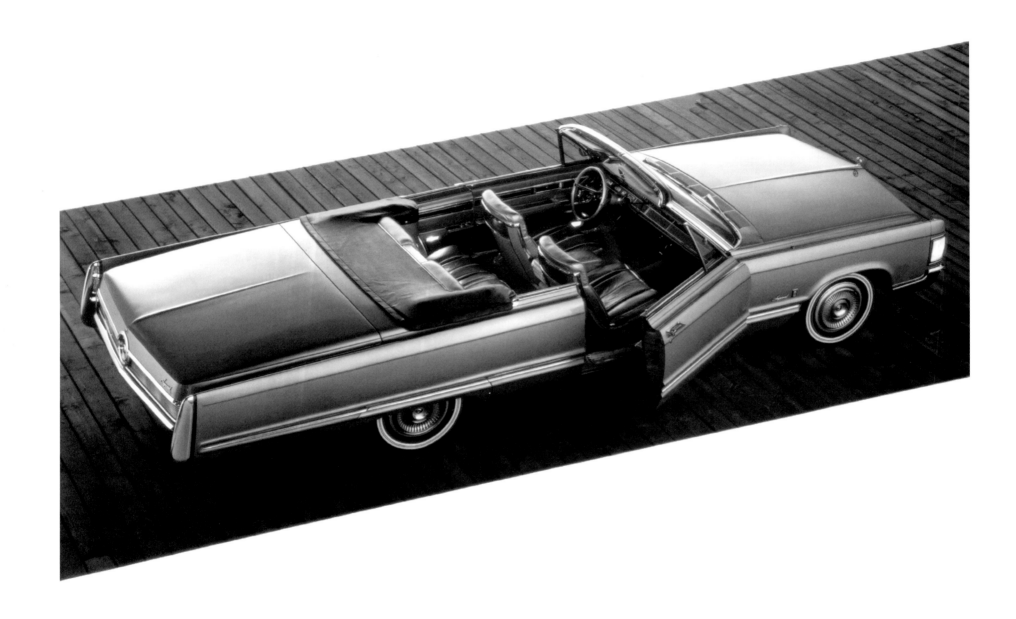

Chrysler Historical Collection

134

1968

IMPERIAL CROWN AND LeBARON

The 1968 Imperial Crown Four Door Hardtop. *Chrysler Historical Collection*

The 1968 Crown Convertible. *Chrysler Historical Collection*

The 1968 LeBaron featured a smaller rear window and padded vinyl roof. *Chrysler Historical Collection*

MODELS AND SERIAL NUMBERS

Year	Model	Chassis Serial Numbers	Unit Production
1964	Imperial Crown—Series VY1-M	9,243,100,001 and up	
	Two Door Hardtop		5,233
	FourDoorHardtop		14,181
	Convertible		922
1964	Imperial LeBaron—Series VY1-H	9,343,100,001 and up	
	Four Door Hardtop		2,949
1965	Imperial Crown—Series AY1-M	Y,253,100,001 and up	
	Two Door Hardtop		3,974
	Four Door Hardtop		11,628
	Convertible		633
1965	Imperial LeBaron—Series AY1-H	Y,353,100,001 and up	
	Four Door Hardtop		2,164
1966	Imperial Crown—Series BY1-M	YM43,J63,100,001 and up; YM23,J63,100,001 and up; YM27,J63,100,001 and up	
	Two Door Hardtop		2,373
	Four Door Hardtop		8,977
	Convertible		514
1966	Imperial LeBaron—Series BY1-H	YH43,J63,100,001 and up	
	Four Door Hardtop		1,878

Year	Model	Chassis Serial Numbers	Unit Production
1967	Imperial Crown—Series CY1-M	YM41,73,100,001 and up; YM43,73,100,001 and up; YM23,73,100,001 and up; YM27,73,100,001 and up	
	Two Door Hardtop		3,235
	Four Door Hardtop		9,415
	Four Door Sedan		2,193
	Convertible		577
1967	Imperial LeBaron—Series CY1-H	YH43,73,100,001 and up	
	Four Door Hardtop		2,194
1968	Imperial Crown—Series DY1-M	YM41,8C,100,001 and up; YM43,8C,100,001 and up; YM23,8C,100,001 and up; YM27,8C,100,001 and up	
	Two Door Hardtop		2,656
	Four Door Hardtop		8,492
	Four Door Sedan		1,887
	Convertible		474
1968	Imperial LeBaron—Series DY1-H	YH43,8C,100,001 and up	
	Four Door Hardtop		1,852

The Iconografix Photo Archive Series includes:

JOHN DEERE MODEL D Photo Archive	ISBN 1-882256-00-X
JOHN DEERE MODEL A Photo Archive	ISBN 1-882256-12-3
JOHN DEERE MODEL B Photo Archive	ISBN 1-882256-01-8
JOHN DEERE 30 SERIES Photo Archive	ISBN 1-882256-13-1
FARMALL REGULAR Photo Archive	ISBN 1-882256-14-X
FARMALL F-SERIES Photo Archive	ISBN 1-882256-02-6
FARMALL MODEL H Photo Archive	ISBN 1-882256-03-4
FARMALL MODEL M Photo Archive	ISBN 1-882256-15-8
CATERPILLAR THIRTY Photo Archive	ISBN 1-882256-04-2
CATERPILLAR SIXTY Photo Archive	ISBN 1-882256-05-0
CATERPILLAR MILITARY TRACTORS VOLUME 1 Photo Archive	ISBN 1-882256-16-6
CATERPILLAR MILITARY TRACTORS VOLUME 2 Photo Archive	ISBN 1-882256-17-4
TWIN CITY TRACTOR Photo Archive	ISBN 1-882256-06-9
MINNEAPOLIS-MOLINE U-SERIES Photo Archive	ISBN 1-882256-07-7
HART-PARR Photo Archive	ISBN 1-882256-08-5
OLIVER TRACTORS Photo Archive	ISBN 1-882256-09-3
HOLT TRACTORS Photo Archive	ISBN 1-882256-10-7
RUSSELL GRADERS Photo Archive	ISBN 1-882256-11-5
MACK MODEL AB Photo Archive	ISBN 1-882256-18-2
MACK MODEL B 1953-66 Photo Archive	ISBN 1-882256-19-0

LE MANS 1950: THE BRIGGS CUNNINGHAM CAMPAIGN Photo Archive	ISBN 1-882256-21-2
SEBRING 12-HOUR RACE 1970 Photo Archive	ISBN 1-882256-20-4
IMPERIAL 1955-1963 Photo Archive	ISBN 1-882256-22-0
IMPERIAL 1964-1968 Photo Archive Available Early 1995	ISBN 1-882256-23-9
STUDEBAKER 1926-1938 Photo Archive	ISBN 1-882256-24-7
STUDEBAKER 1939-1958 Photo Archive	ISBN 1-882256-25-5
GORDON BENNETT CUP 1905 Postcard Archive	ISBN 1-882256-26-3
AMERICAN SERVICE STATIONS 1935-1943 Photo Archive	ISBN 1-882256-27-1
MACK FC, FCSW & NW1936-1947 Photo Archive	ISBN 1-882256-28-X
MACK EB, EC, ED, EE, EF, EG & DE 1936-1951 Photo Archive	ISBN 1-882256-29-8
INTERNATIONAL TD CRAWLERS Photo Archive	ISBN 1-882256-30-1
FARMALL EXPERIMENTAL TRACTORS Photo Archive	ISBN 1-882256-31-X
CASE TRACTORS Photo Archive	ISBN 1-882256-32-8
FORDSON 1917-1928 Photo Archive	ISBN 1-882256-33-6

The Iconografix Photo Archive Series is available from direct mail specialty book dealers and bookstores throughout the world, or can be ordered from the publisher.

For information write to:
Iconografix
P.O. Box 609
Osceola, Wisconsin 54020 USA

Telephone: (715) 294-2792
(800) 289-3504 (USA and Canada)
Fax: (715) 294-3414